Theseus and the Minotaur: The History o
Famous Leg

By Andrew Scott & Charles River Editors

A depiction of Rhea

About Charles River Editors

Charles River Editors is a boutique digital publishing company, specializing in bringing history back to life with educational and engaging books on a wide range of topics. Keep up to date with our new and free offerings with [this 5 second sign up on our weekly mailing list](), and visit [Our Kindle Author Page]() to see other recently published Kindle titles.

We make these books for you and always want to know our readers' opinions, so we encourage you to leave reviews and look forward to publishing new and exciting titles each week.

Introduction

Theseus and Aethra, **by Laurent de La Hyre**

Theseus and the Minotaur

"Theseus, the hero-slayer of the Minotaur, entered Crete from without, as the symbol and arm of the rising civilisation of the Greeks." - Joseph Campbell[1]

Countless civilizations have come and gone over the course of time, but interest in mythology is one of the great constants. People have approached myths from countless angles, some denigrating and self-righteous, others earnest and open-minded, but there is something mystical and universal in all myths that speaks to the reader across the years, regardless of what they know of historiography or "schools of thought."

The truth is that all of these stories live in a murky, anachronistic history so entangled that trying to unravel it can mean everything or nothing at all. One of the reasons for this is the age of most myths, especially those from ancient times (the name Theseus can be traced back as far as 1450 BCE, for instance). Another is the sheer volume of possible versions there can be of a

---

[1] Campbell 2008 p. 12

given myth.

A lot of mythological stories span centuries, so it's likely that nothing like an "original version" of Theseus and the Minotaur will ever be known. In fact, even if the story could be traced all the way back, the "original" is likely to be so far removed from the beloved modern-day version that it would not be adopted as canon anyway. Nor, it has to be said, can a version of the story be isolated that would have been read at a specific point in time, such as the Classical Period, since a lot of the sources for stories like Theseus are either fragmentary or come even later. Moreover, an "original" is less important than the layers of meaning accumulated over the ages. To the modern reader, the sum of the parts can be more fruitful than the mode of conception.

Regardless, as one of the most famous myths of all time, the story of Theseus has been at the heart of Greek mythology since he became Athens' "Culture Hero" at the beginning of the 5th century BCE, and variants on his story surface in countless ancient sources. The importance of the story to the Greeks themselves makes it worth looking at the story from a historical standpoint; many scholars believe the actions and events in myths have a basis in historical fact. On the other hand, Joseph Campbell's "monomyth" theory takes a different approach by suggesting all myths are part of a wider, mythological framework representing the psychological needs of the reader.

Whether the approaches are "correct" has been and will continue to be debated in scholarly circles for the foreseeable future, but in many respects both sides of the debate can add value and understanding for modern readers. Even in the case of a story like Theseus that so many people are familiar with, studying the legend allows for different ways of interpreting it, and helps readers understand all the different variations of events within it.

Theseus and the Minotaur: The History of One of Greek Mythology's Most Famous Legends looks at the myth of Theseus and the Minotaur, based on both Greek and Roman sources, from which both fascinating and key elements of the story emerge. Along with pictures depicting important people, places, and events, you will learn about the story like never before.

Theseus and the Minotaur: The History of One of Greek Mythology's Most Famous Legends
About Charles River Editors
Introduction
   The Story
   The History of the Culture Hero
   Crete
   The Labyrinth
   Cult
   The Moon-Goddess
   The Meaning
   Online Resources
   Bibliography
Free Books by Charles River Editors
Discounted Books by Charles River Editors

The Story

The Birth of the Minotaur

The story of Theseus and the Minotaur begins with the "passions" of Zeus, as so many stories in Greek mythology do. The city of Tyre, on the coast of what was then Phoenicia, was once the seat of a mighty kingdom. The beauty of its architecture was famed across the known world and that of its princess, even more so. The daughter of King Agenor was called Europa, and though she didn't know it at the time, the events of her life would give birth to a continent and an immortal story.

Europa was the granddaughter of Poseidon, but this did not assuage the lustful attentions of the sea-god's brother. When Zeus saw the beautiful Europa, he summoned Hermes to his lofty home and ordered him to travel to Tyre to convince King Agenor to graze his herd of cattle, down by the sea. The messenger god did so, and as the cattle were grazing, Zeus emerged from the sea in the form of a resplendent white bull, and ambled into the herd. The young princess, who regularly took walks along the shore with her attendants, arrived at her father's herd of cattle and was immediately captivated by the beauty of this perfectly white beast. She hesitated at first, preferring to keep her distance in case it was as hostile as it was handsome, but Zeus played his part with perfection, and Europa soon drew closer. Approaching it, she stroked its horns and hide, and soon she dared to mount its broad back and amble into the shallows. The shallows grew deeper, but the white bull didn't slow at the swells or the crested whitecaps of the open sea; it slowed only when it had reached the shores of Gortyna on the isle of Crete. There, Zeus transformed again and ravaged the young Phoenician princess.

A painting of Europa and the bull by Jean Francois de Troy

Europa bore three sons to the king of the gods: Sarpedon, Rhadamanthys, and Minos, and when Zeus returned to his wife on Mount Olympus, she married the local ruler, Asterius, who adopted Europa's divine children and made her queen. They lived and ruled, and their sons grew to be wise and doting children.

When King Asterius died, however, the lure of a young boy strained the fraternal bonds. Sarpedon, Rhadamanthys, and Minos all fell in love with the young boy, Miletus, and when the boy chose Sarpedon as his favorite, Minos had him exiled to the land that would later bear his name and announced himself sole ruler of Crete. Sarpedon insisted that the island–which Minos had already divided into three–be ruled equally between the brothers. Minos disagreed and condemned Sarpedon to the same fate as his beloved. Rhadamanthys, wiser and less aspiring than his brother, governed his third under the patronage of Minos, and he lived a long and prosperous life.

The successor of King Agenor amassed a great naval empire throughout the Mediterranean and soon chose Pasiphaë, daughter of Helios, the Sun, for his wife. In a declaration of his divine right to rule, he proclaimed the gods would answer whatever prayer he offered them. After making all of the necessary preparations for a sacrifice and dedicating an altar to Poseidon, he asked for a bull to sacrifice in honor of the god. Shortly, a white bull so beautiful it could rival the one that spirited his mother away appeared from the surf and presented itself to the new king. It pained Minos to kill such a divine specimen, and so he summoned the most beautiful, white bull he had in his herd and sacrificed that instead, choosing to keep Poseidon's offering for himself. But the gods didn't abide insults such as this easily, and the hubris of Minos would soon be repaid with brutal severity.

Minos committed no such act of hubris towards Zeus, however, and the lord of gods gave him a prize on his ascension to the throne of Crete. Zeus sent Minos the bull-headed bronze servant, Talos, to guard his island. Talos ran the coast of Crete three times a day, throwing enormous rocks at any foreign ships that came near, and every three years, he would enter the inland villages and bring them news of the laws decreed by their King on brazen tablets. Once, when the Sardinians mustered the audacity to attack Minos's imperial center, Talos saw that his rocks could no longer hold the fleet at bay, so he changed his tactic. Immersing himself in a fire until his bronze body gleamed red hot, he ran at the Sardinian ships that had landed ashore and wrapped each in his searing embrace until they broke into flames, grinning in bovine malice as he did. Some say this is the origin of the term "sardonic grin."[2]

Before this had happened, Minos had accepted the great inventor, Daedalus (perhaps best known as the father of Icarus), into the capital city Knossos after he was exiled from his native Athens for a crime of passion. "Daedalus belonged to the royal Athenian clan called the Metionidae, and he was rather famous among all men not only for his art but also for his wandering and his misfortunes. For he killed his sister's son, and knowing the customs of his city he went into exile of his own accord to Minos in Crete."[3] The ability of this great craftsman was celebrated throughout Athens and beyond. He was known to have delighted the royal family by creating small, animated, wooden dolls that were so lifelike they were almost divine.

---

[2] Graves 1955
[3] Pausanias VII 4. 5

Frederick Leighton's painting of Daedalus and Icarus

It was to Daedalus, however, that Queen Pasiphaë turned when in the grip of a divinely sent, unspeakable lust for the very white bull her husband had failed to sacrifice to Poseidon. Thankful for his treatment in exile, Daedalus was loathe to refuse the Queen's requests and employed the skills he'd learned at the hands of Athena herself to create a dazzling hollow cow the divine bull would not be able to resist. He showed Pasiphaë how to enter the hollow facsimile of a cow, slide her legs into the straps he'd built into the hindquarters, and left her to wait among the herd. Soon, Poseidon's bull mounted the wooden cow and the Queen's lust was sated. After this, her belly swelled, and she gave birth to a monstrous creature, half human and with the head of a bull, whom she named Asterius.

An ancient Etruscan depiction of Pasiphaë and the Minotaur

Returning from visiting his 90 island cities and ridding the sea of pirates, Minos found the monstrosity his wife had birthed, and which was now his burden by divine law: the "Minotaur." Not knowing what to do, he sought advice from an oracle. "In obedience, Minos kept him enclosed in the Labyrinth. This Labyrinth, which Daedalus had constructed, was a building 'that with a maze of winding ways confused the passage out.'"[4]

However, when he learned it was that same, great Athenian who had contrived the apparatus his wife had used in her bestiality, Minos threw Daedalus into the very labyrinth he had built, along with his own wife and her shameful son.

The Birth of Theseus

Aegeus, King of Athens, found himself unable to father a son with his first or second wife, so as any concerned Athenian would, he traveled to the Oracle at Delphi and inquired as to what he

---
[4] Apollodorus' Library III.1.4

should do to remedy his apparent infertility. As was the Oracle's way, the response was cryptic and seemingly unconnected:

> "The bulging mouth of the wineskin, most excellent of men,
>
> Untie it not until you have arrived at the height of Athens."

Not knowing how to interpret the vision and unable to request another, Aegeus set down the mountain and returned home. On his way to Athens, he stopped at Corinth. It was there he met Medea, formidable mistress of herbs and tinctures, who asked him for a suspicious favor: "Swear an oath that you'll protect me from all enemies in the event of me seeking shelter in your great city and I will employ all magic, all skill in brewing tonics from divine plants in procuring for you a son." Aegeus agreed and left the city at the Isthmus of Troezen.

In the city of Troezen, the king rejoiced in feasts with his old friends, Pittheus and Troezen. As it happened, Pittheus, too, was in a state of lament for his daughter, Aethra, because she had been betrothed to the great hero Bellerophon but had to cancel the wedding when he was sent away from the city in disgrace. "Pittheus, grasping the sense of the oracle, made Aegeus drunk and ensured that he went to bed with his daughter, Aethra."[5] And so, with the help of flowing wine and the far-reaching effects of Medea's magic, Aegeus awoke the next morning to find himself in exactly that position.

Aethra, however, had not been at his side the entire night. She had woken in the middle of her slumber after having a dream sent to her by Athena. The dream told her to leave her drunken lover and wade into the waters until she reached the nearby island of Sphaeria. The goddess charged her with bringing libations to the tomb of Sphaerus, who had been Pelops' charioteer during the Trojan War, but before she could reach the tomb she was overpowered by the god Poseidon, who emerged from the waves and ravished her in the night.

Aegeus was unaware of this night-time encounter with the god, and though he had little hope of Aethra becoming pregnant, he was still mindful of Medea's power and her promise to do all she could in order to bestow a son upon him. For this reason, he gave Aethra orders not to expose any son that may be born to her, nor send him to be raised in another city. Instead, she was to raise the boy in secret in Troezen, and when the time came, if the strength of the boy's arm was matched by his tenacity, then he would find a mighty stone on the road from Troezen to Athens named the Altar of Strong Zeus. If he was strong enough to lift it, the boy would find his father's sword and sandals beneath the stone, which the boy subsequently had to bring to Athens to prove his birth. With this announcement, Aegeus once again padded the dusty road home and placed the tokens beneath the rock that only he and Heracles were capable of lifting.

Aethra gave birth to Theseus in Troezen and raised the boy in secret with the help of her father.

---

[5] Apollodorus' Library III.15.6

Pittheus discretely spread the rumor that the boy's true father was Poseidon, because if his true identity were to become known, a war of succession amongst Aegeus's 50 nephews would break out and likely cause the young boy's death.

Theseus grew into a valiant and precocious young boy who first displayed his valor at the age of 7, when his cousin Heracles came to visit his grandfather, Pittheus. "One day, Heracles, dining at Troezen with Pittheus, removed his lion-skin and threw it over a stool. When the palace children came in, they screamed and fled, all except seven-year-old Theseus, who ran to snatch an axe from the woodpile, and returned boldly, prepared to attack a real lion."[6]

16 years had passed since Aethra had lain with her two lovers, and the boy had grown in valiance, strength, and guile. While on a trip to the Oracle at Delphi, his mother showed him the rock of the Altar of Strong Zeus and told him the true story of his birth. Delighted at the chance to prove himself, Theseus sprung to his feet and lifted the rock with ease, and in that instant, he knew that he was destined for greatness. He told his mother that he would set out in search of his father, ridding the treacherous path along the way of the infamous bandits and ne'er-do-wells infesting it. His mother's pleas for him to take the safer route by sea echoed against the huge boulder, henceforth called the "Rock of Theseus," and dissipated into the ether.

The Road to Athens

---

[6] Graves 1955 p.325

Kodros Painter's picture of ancient depictions of the deeds of Theseus

Young Theseus hoped to emulate the great feats of his cousin Heracles on this road, and so he promised, though he would not choose a quarrel with anybody, he would rid the road of criminals and make their punishment fit their crimes. He first met the murderous Periphetes, who reveled in bludgeoning travelers with his huge club. Theseus lithely avoided his blows, disarmed Periphetes, and caved his head in with the very cudgel with which he had terrorized travelers. Weighing it in his hands, he was delighted with the club and adopted it as his weapon of choice thenceforth.

Next, he met the cruel Sinis, also known as "Pityocamptes," or "Pine-Bender," for his wicked method of murder. Sinis was as strong as a demigod and enjoyed pulling down the tops of pine trees and entreating passersby to help in his strange diversion. If the travelers were kind enough to help, Sinis would do one of two things: either hand them the top of the bent pine, and once they took it, release the tree, sending the poor soul flying into the air to meet their death on some distant ground; or tie their arms and legs to two bent pines which he would then release and render the wayfarer in two. Theseus chose the bloody latter as his punishment for the wicked Sinis.

At Crommyum, Theseus came upon a murderous sow that had been plaguing the lands and killing the farmers at their work. "Now the Crommyonian sow, which they called Phaea, was no insignificant creature, but fierce and hard to master. This sow he went out of his way to encounter and slay, that he might not be thought to perform all his exploits under compulsion, and at the same time because he thought that while the brave man ought to attack villainous men only in self defense, he should seek occasion to risk his life in battle with the nobler beasts. However, some say that Phaea was a female robber, a woman of murderous and unbridled spirit, who dwelt in Crommyon, was called Sow because of her life and manners, and was afterwards slain by Theseus."[7]

---

[7] Plutarch *Theseus* 9

An ancient depiction of Theseus and the Crommyonian sow

Further along the road, he came to some formidable cliffs where the trail became narrow and treacherous. The cliffs rose from the waves to a high zenith where the bandit, Sciron, made his base. Sciron would feign weakness and beg travelers to stoop and wash his feet. Once they were stooped in a merciful crouch, Sciron would only have to push slightly to send the traveler in a deadly arc over the edge of the cliff to the crashing swells below, where a vicious turtle waited to devour them. Wise to the bandit's trickery, Theseus refused to wash Sciron's feet and lifted him from his rock to toss him over the cliff to meet the same fate as his victims instead.

It wasn't his strength that aided the young hero in his next encounter with banditry but his talent for stratagem. He met the Arcadian bandit, Cercyon, who challenged passersby to wrestle him, trusting his superhuman strength to secure victory for himself and a bloody end for his combatant. Theseus, however, did not try to equal Cercyon's strength but instead evaded his murderous grip with an agile leap, darted toward the bandit's knees, lifted him up in the air, and flung his head speeding downward to dash his brains on the rocks.

The last bandit Theseus met on the road to Athens was Polypemon, son of pine-bending Sinis. Polypemon had a house on the road with spare rooms he offered to weary travelers. They say he had only two beds in these rooms, and he would allocate one or the other according to the height of his guest. If the guest was short, he would make ready the long bed and rack his visitor until he fit, or more often, be torn asunder. If the guest was tall, Polypemon would make ready the short bed and saw off whatever of his legs protruded from the end. Theseus exacted his punishment accordingly.

Murder is the ultimate sin, but any sin can be wiped clean, so when Theseus arrived in Attica, he met the sons of Phytalus, who purified his blood by letting in the River Cephissus. This allowed him to enter the city of his father absolved, and when he arrived, he found that the powerful Medea had been forced from Corinth and had invoked the oath Aegeus had taken to shelter her if ever she were in need. Aegeus had left his wife and married the exiled enchantress with the hope her magic would finally award him an heir.

Although the king was unaware of the birth of Theseus, Medea was not, and when she saw the dashing young hero enter the city, she feared for the fate of her young son Medus, who she hoped would succeed his father, Aegeus, to the Athenian throne. Medea convinced Aegeus Theseus was a spy sent by some enemy, and if he invited him to a feast at the Dolphin Temple, she could prepare a tincture from poisonous wolfsbane to do away with him. However, when the young man came to dinner, Aegeus spied the detail of the Erechtheid serpents inlaid on the hilt of his own sword and swiped at the cup just before it met his son's lips. The poison glistened on the temple floor as Medea and Medus fled Theseus's revenge, draped in a magical cloud.

Aegeus, the proud father, listened as his heroic son regaled him with tales of his labors on the road from Troezen to Athens, but the festivities were cut short when Aegeus's nephews revolted, questioning the legitimacy of this new son. 25 of them laid siege to the city, while the other 25 lay in ambush nearby. Already beloved by the populace, Theseus was given prior knowledge of the ambush, and he employed his great intelligence to foil their plans. By the time the ambush had been defeated and Theseus had threatened the besieging force, the remaining nephews had surrendered.

The Wrath of Minos

Before he could glory in his victory, Theseus heard of a marauding, fire-breathing bull Heracles had brought from Crete that was terrorizing the plains of Attica. It had killed many men from the Isthmus of Marathon, one of whom was Minos's own son, Androgeus. Years earlier, Androgeus had made his name as a great athlete, competing in games organized by King Aegeus. Rather than showering the youth in praise, Aegeus was jealous of the son of a great king and told him that if he believed himself worthy, he would tackle the real challenge of the "Bull of Marathon." Androgeus rose to the challenge, but his ability did not match his ambition. "When he was let loose on the Argive plain he fled through the [I]sthmus of Corinth, into the land of Attica as far as the Attic parish of Marathon, killing all he met, including Androgeus, son of Minos. Minos sailed against Athens with a fleet, not believing that the Athenians were innocent of the death of Androgeus, and sorely harassed them until it was agreed that he should take seven maidens and seven boys for the Minotaur that was said to dwell in the Labyrinth at Knossos."[8]

---

[8] Pausanias I. 27. 10

Theseus made short work of the fire-breathing bull and paraded its fearsome corpse through the streets of Athens, but the wrath of Minos was soon to envelope the new hero in a way that would define his legacy from then on.

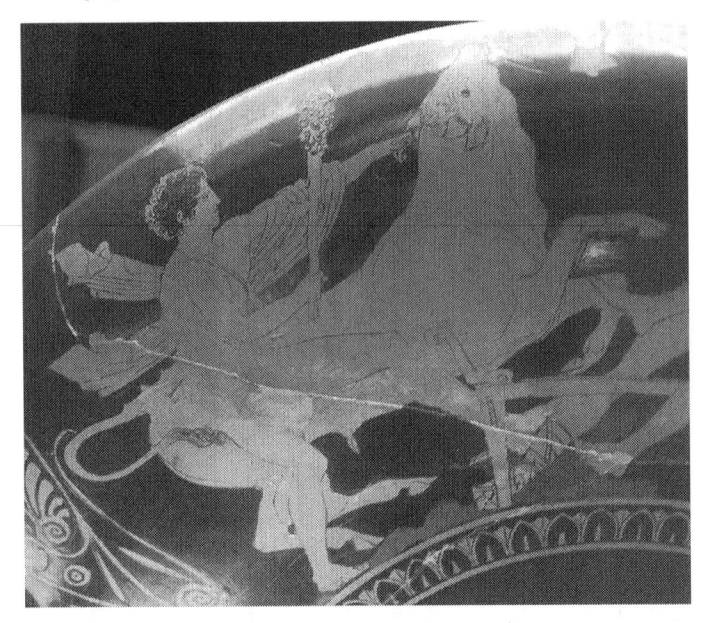

Luis Garcia's picture of an ancient depiction of Theseus and the bull

Theseus arrived in Athens at the close of the third Great Year since the death of Minos's son, Androgeus. The Great Year came around every nine years, and Theseus was about to witness the deadly tribute Minos demanded in his wrath. Either taking pity on the Athenian mothers or thirsty for further chances to prove his worthiness as a hero, Theseus volunteered to be one of the boys offered to the Minotaur. His foresight matched his cunning, though, and in the weeks before his departure for Crete, he selected and trained two other boys to learn how to walk, talk, and assume all of the general characteristics of a typical Athenian girl their age, thereby arranging for them to take the place of two girls on the black-sailed ship.

On the day of departure, Aegeus wept for his son and begged him one last time to allow another boy–chosen by lot, as was the custom–to take his place, but Theseus would not let his father's tears assuage his fervor for glory, and he embarked for Crete. He did, however, accept a white sail from his father, which he promised to unfurl in the likelihood of his successful return from the dreaded labyrinth at Knossos.

Before he had left, the Oracle at Delphi had advised Theseus to bring Aphrodite with him as a companion on his voyage, as she was prepared to offer her divine aid, but only if he asked for it. Thus, as the black ship approached the island, Theseus made a sacrifice to the image of Aphrodite he had brought with him.

Once the ship arrived at the shore, Minos was there to ensure his tribute. While counting his offerings, he was struck by the beauty of an Athenian maiden, whom he would have ravaged right there on the shore in front of her countrymen had it not been for Theseus's intervention. The Cretan King was a voracious seducer of women and nymphs during his rule, never letting his advances be spurned by anyone, even those who feared for their lives. "Minos'[s] many infidelities so enraged Pasiphaë that she put a spell upon him: whenever he lay with another woman he discharged, not seeds, but a swarm of noxious serpents, scorpions, and millipedes, which preyed on her vitals."[9] He was about to ravish the girl when Theseus called out that it was his duty as the son of Poseidon to protect virgins from the advances of tyrants. The king laughed at this arrogant youth and threw his golden signet ring into the sea. "As far as I know Poseidon never shied away from ravaging any virgins who took his fancy but if you *are* the son of the god then prove it by retrieving this ring from the dark depths." Theseus challenged the king, to first prove that *he* was a son of Zeus as he claimed, to which Minos replied with a prayer to his father that was answered at once with the clapping of thunder and blazes of lightning.

Theseus was left with no choice other than to retrieve the king's ring. As he went into the sea, he was escorted by a school of dolphins to the palace of the Nereids, the sea nymphs whose queen was Thetis, the daughter of the Titans and the mother of Achilles. She gave the hero the signet ring he sought and also a jeweled crown to take back with him to the surface.

The Oracle at Delphi was proven right again when Theseus emerged from the sea with his prizes. Amongst the throngs of Cretans occupying the shore was Minos and Pasiphaë's only daughter, Ariadne. She had been in charge of the Labyrinth for most of her life, organizing and ensuring correct preparations for sacrifices dedicated to Poseidon in recompense for her father's earlier transgression.

Graceful and charming, she stood transfixed by the youth who challenged her tyrannical father's lust. She jostled through the retreating crowd toward the Athenian youths as they walked in a train toward the quarters where they would await their fate, one by one. Whether thanks to the help of Aphrodite or simply her own cunning, Ariadne succeeded in drawing close enough to Theseus to whisper in his ear: "'I will help you kill my half-brother, the Minotaur,' she secretly promised him, 'if I may return to Athens with you as your wife.' The offer Theseus gladly accepted, and swore to marry her. Now, before Daedalus escaped Crete with Pasiphaë's help, he had given Ariadne a magic ball of thread, and instructed her how to enter and leave the Labyrinth. She must open the entrance door and tie the loose end of the thread to the lintel; the ball would then roll along, diminishing as it went and making, with devious turns and twists, for

---

[9] Graves 1955 p. 299, Antoninus *Metamorphoses* 41

the inner most recess where the Minotaur was lodged. The ball Ariadne gave to Theseus, and instructed him to follow it until he reached the sleeping monster, whom he must seize by the hair and sacrifice to Poseidon. He could then find his way back by rolling up the thread into a ball again."[10]

It is said that, in return for this magic ball and as a way of endowing his promise of marriage to Ariadne with divine assertion, Theseus gave her the jeweled crown he retrieved from Thetis under the sea.

Soon came Theseus's moment of sacrifice. He stood before the looming walls of the labyrinth, and though his heart raced with the magnitude of his greatest test of valor yet, he kept the clarity of mind to fix the beginning of his magical thread to the outermost lintel and follow it to his destiny. He marched forward each time he heard the muffled snorts and garbled roars of the dreaded Minotaur within. The guards had stripped him of the club he took from Sinis, and Ariadne had been unable to bring him any other weapons, so he knew he had to defeat the Minotaur as his cousin had defeated the Nemean lion: with his bare hands.

He reached the center and placed down the ball of thread that had magically resisted unwinding fully, despite the great distance over which it had guided the hero. The Minotaur charged out of the recesses of the inner sanctum and Theseus leapt at it. He employed every ounce of his nerve and utilized every sinew of stratagem to outwit the beast until he succeeded in wrestling it down with his own hands, holding it there until its final breath had been snuffed out.

---

[10] Graves 1955 p. 339, Plutarch *Theseus* 19

A Roman mosaic depicting Theseus and the Minotaur in the Labyrinth

Ancient art depicting Theseus and the Minotaur

Theseus emerged at night and was greeted at the entrance by his betrothed. Ariadne led him to the jail where the other prisoners had been kept, arriving to find that the two disguised boys had killed their guards and freed the other would-be victims. They reached the harbor and sabotaged as much of the Cretan fleet as possible before boarding their ship and setting sail for Athens in the moonlight.

Some days later, they stopped at the island of Naxos in the Cyclades. They stocked up on what few provisions they lacked and made due sacrifices and preparations for their return, but Theseus was compelled to make the first mistake in all his labors. While Ariadne slept on the island, he gave the order to leave her behind. When she awoke realizing she'd been betrayed, she called upon the gods. "Is it thus, O perfidious, when dragged from my motherland's shores, is it thus, O false Theseus, that you leave me on this desolate strand? Thus do you depart unmindful of slighted godheads, bearing home your perjured vows? Was no thought able to bend the intent of your ruthless mind? Had you no clemency there, that your pitiless bowels might show me compassion? But these were not the promises you gave me idly of old, this was not what you bade me hope for, but the blithe bride-bed, hymenaeal happiness: all empty air, blown away by the breezes. Now, now, let no woman give credence to man's oath, let none hope for faithful vows from mankind; for while their eager desire strives for its end, nothing fear they to swear, nothing of promises forbear they: but instantly their lusting thoughts are satiate with lewdness, nothing of speech they remember, nothing of perjuries care. In truth I snatched you from the midst of the whirlpool of death, preferring to suffer the loss of a brother rather than fail your need in the supreme hour, O ingrate…O goddesses, may he bring evil on himself and on his kin."[11]

    Theseus continued his journey home, stopping at the small island of Delos, where he sacrificed to Apollo and celebrated athletic games in his honor. He introduced the "Crane" dance here, a dance he'd learned during his imprisonment in Knossos, which consisted of measured steps in labyrinthine movements atop an ornate floor. Theseus and his crewmates all performed this dance at a temple it was said Apollo had built himself, and after honoring the god, they continued on their way to Athens.

    As Theseus approached the port of his father's city, Ariadne's prayer was answered. The gods had doused the sailors' minds with a fog of forgetfulness while at sea, and the white sail Aegeus had given him to unfurl if he were successful lay forgotten below the deck. Aegeus had waited on the Acropolis for his son since he had boarded the ship, and when he saw the black sail curled in the wind, he took this as a sign of Theseus's failure and threw himself off the precipice to his death below.

    Theseus succeeded his father as king of Athens, but his labors, trials, and adventures didn't cease when he ascended the throne. He fought Amazons, joined the hunt for the Calydonian Boar, and escaped eternal damnation in the Underworld, but it was his adventure with the Minotaur that cemented his fame, and the death of his father afforded him pity.

The History of the Culture Hero

    The study of myth is one of mankind's most beloved and fruitful endeavors, and there are about as many ways of approaching these stories as there are scholars prepared to approach them. Some approach myths as fables, pretty lessons for future generations, while others discover the basis of ritual and religious practice amidst the battles and the banal. Each method, no matter how extensive the study, is flawed and inevitably winnows out more gold dust than it

---

[11] Catullus *Carmina* 64

hopes to keep in its pan.

However, that is no reason to abandon the study as a "lost cause." Each reader will mine from a story what they need if they enjoy the process, and one of the more enjoyable methods is that of studying myth as a blurred record of historical fact. Robert Graves, the poet, novelist, and renowned classicist, was a keen practitioner of this method, and his footnotes to *The Greek Myths* have been analyzed extensively for this interpretation of Theseus's life leading up to his duel with the Minotaur. According to Graves, in addition to being the shadows of memories, myths were almost conscious constructions of propaganda and politically important genealogies by the mythographers who eventually recorded them.

Everything in the myth of Theseus pertains to power. Every divine visit and mortal misdemeanor represents the worn-down edges of a distant memory, foggy and transmogrified by the passage of time, having been handled by many hands. The outside walls of the Parthenon in Athens, were lined with four sets of continuous friezes, divided into panels called metopes. These friezes showed the great battles in Hellenic history as the ancients perceived it. There is the Titanomachy (the war between the Gods and the Titans), the Amazonomachy (the war between the Greeks and the Amazons), the Gigantomachy (the war between the Gods and the Giants), and the Centauromachy. Theseus can be found at the center of the Centauromachy, as it was at his best friend's wedding that he was forced to do battle against the Centaurs, who had gone mad with lust after imbibing wine. All of these magnificent pieces of art figuratively represent Athens' victory (it is, after all, propaganda of the finest quality) over the "barbaric" Persian Empire in the early 5th century BCE. It was during this time of war and invasion that Theseus was elevated to a position of extreme importance in Athenian culture, becoming their national "Culture Hero."

How does a young man born at Troezen become the national hero nearly 100 miles away at Athens? The key to this adoption arrives on the night of his conception. Graves suggests that Theseus may have had a twin at one point, as this was the norm for heroes whose mothers slept with two "men" on the night of their conception. In the case of Theseus, however, he didn't need a twin as much as he needed an Athenian father, and so the twin became a vestigial friend whose provenance was provided in the form of the drunken and spellbound Aegeus on the road from Delphi. The fact that the mythographers chose Troezen as Aethra's birthplace could very well be the remnants of some contemporary propaganda, since Athens had a "real-world" connection with this city throughout the Bronze Age and beyond.[12] As unlikely as it may seem, peace treaties were brokered in ancient Greece and mercy given on the basis of shared heritage and mythological connections, so this projection of diplomatic relations upon an old story may not be as far-fetched as it first appears.

His parentage established Theseus as having been "of Athens," but this was not spectacular

---

[12] 1955 p.326

enough to warrant his promotion to "hero status." For that, the mythographers needed Poseidon to ravish Aethra on the same night she lay with Aegeus. With this possibility of divine conception, Theseus's strength and cunning could surge to superhuman levels, allowing him to call upon the name of the god whenever he wished, as in the case of his protection of the virgin on the Cretan shore, an episode that pits one "divinely favored" hero against another.

Interestingly, Theseus's discovery of the "tokens" left for him beneath the immovable stone is not simply a sign of his divinely endowed physical strength (as often emphasised in modern mythology books) but instead a sign of his divine royalty. As Graves points out, "Sandals and sword are ancient symbols of royalty; the drawing of a sword from a rock seems to have formed part of the Bronze Age coronation ritual. Odin, Galahad, and Arthur were all in turn required to perform a similar feat."[13] In one fell swoop, at the age of 16, Theseus is given the heritage and right of a royal Athenian and shown the way to his destiny.

With this, Theseus had taken another step toward becoming a "Culture Hero," but the mythographers still needed to instill within him the aspects of might and valiance that are so important to the role. For this reason, throughout his story, Theseus is held up against Heracles, the greatest of all ancient Greek heroes. From his labors to the club taken from him in his moment of need at Knossos, Theseus is favorably compared to his "cousin" in almost all sources, serving to elevate the city and people of Athens to a recognizably grandiose position in the ancient Greek psyche.

Crete

Sir Arthur Evans was an English archaeologist who won fame for unearthing the palace at Knossos and (liberally) embroidering his archaeology with a fervent love of mythology. During the 19th and early 20th centuries, sober archaeologists adamantly believed in their capability of discovering the lands and battlefields they had read about in their classical education. Archaeologist Heinrich Schliemann dug at Troy and other sites in the late 19th century BCE, invariably labeling the sites he excavated as being those mentioned in the works of Homer. He "discovered" the "Jewels of Helen" amidst "Priam's Treasure" and the death mask he claimed to have belonged to that great mythological commander, Agamemnon, at Mycenae. In doing so, he discovered the real, late Bonze Age Greek culture known today as the "Mycenaean Civilization" (c.1600-1100 BCE).

---

[13] ibid.

Evans

Sir Arthur Evans later realized that his excavations had unearthed another civilization, one that predated Schliemann's "Mycenaean" culture by centuries and used a form of writing now referred to as "Linear A," still yet to be translated. Evans had discovered what is now known as the "Minoan Civilization" (c. 3650 - 1400 BCE), and he painted it with flourishes no less fantastic than Schliemann did at Troy.

Although Evans' research has been disputed–and in some cases refuted–in modern times, there are certain academic assertions he made that are still maintained. For example, the name "Minos" appears in Linear B script–a later, translated form of Linear A–generally considered today to be a state title of some kind translatable as "king" or "warlord," rather than that of a particular ruler. The reasoning behind this abstract translation is due to the fact that the order of succession in Minoan culture was matrilineal. Scholars believe the "queen-priestess" would have chosen her "king," who would have adopted the name "Minos" and its derivatives as her "second in command." "Minos" was his title, and it denoted a very specific function in society.

The king (or "Minos") and queen in Minoan society were the highest-ranking priest and priestess in the state religion. This meant that their union was both political and religious in nature. In the story of the Minotaur, Minos was unfaithful to Pasiphaë on several occasions with "nymphs." Robert Graves believes this episode in the story may have had crucial historical significance. Graves defines this infidelity not in the same sense as those indecencies of Zeus but instead connects them to what is known today as the "Cretan Confederacy."[14] In the myth, Theseus Minos is recorded visiting "his 90 island cities" while his wife gave birth to the Minotaur. This is a reference to the enormous empire the Cretans amassed during the Minoan period. There is reason to believe that Minos's visits to his cities, combined with his apparent infidelity, represent the actual power structure under Minoan rule. Since the queen was not just a queen but also a priestess who was divine in her own right, her ritual marriage to the Minos was a form of unifying the various cities in the Confederacy. Just as princes and princesses were married off to form alliances in the Middle Ages, the "Minos" went through a ritual marriage with each of the cities swearing allegiance to his "divine queen" at Knossos.

Greece was "Cretanized," as Graves calls it, some time in the 18th century BCE. The Cretan empire incorporated cities into its fold with alarming speed, but it was no "velvet revolution." Cities resisted and revolted, the evidence of which can be found in this myth. The story of the death of Minos's son Androgeus, for instance, appears to be a replica of a common mythological trope used to represent the cause of hostilities between two peoples. In fact, Graves goes even further in his historiographical assertions by referring to an alternative episode in the myth of Theseus at Crete, which describes the mythological labyrinth as being a real area within the palace at Knossos.[15] He believes the story of Theseus entering this maze and encountering a hostile force inside represents an actual Athenian raid on the palace at Knossos in which they struggled to find their way through the labyrinthine structures of the palace. Furthermore, the reference to Talos and the Sardinians is a reference to documented Minoan skirmishes with the people of Sardinia and Sicily around this time, which would have made the raid on Knossos much more viable for the Athenians.[16]

The dynastic name, "Minos," refers to a dynasty that had a "Sky Bull" as its emblem, and even a cursory reading of the myth reveals it is laden with fitting symbolism. The story includes the abduction of Europa to the lust of Pasiphaë, the gift of the bull-headed "Talos" from Zeus, the fire-breathing "Bull of Marathon" and the ultimate symbol of the palace at Knossos, the Minotaur itself. The local king–who married Europa and adopted her children–was named "Asterius," which Graves defines as either "of the sun" or "of the sky," and this was also the name given to the "bull creature" at the center of the maze.

---

[14] 1955 p.301
[15] 1955 p.345
[16] ibid.

According to Graves, the term "Minotaur" is actually a mutation of two names, "Minos" and "Taurus," effectively meaning "Minos's Bull." Graves states this was no mystical creature but that "Taurus" was actually the leading Cretan commander whom Theseus "wrestled" and defeated in order to relieve his city of the crushing tribute it had been forced to pay. "Cretans do not admit [the story of the Labyrinth], but declare that the Labyrinth was a dungeon, with no other inconvenience than that its prisoners could not escape; and that Minos instituted funeral games in honor of Androgeus, and as prizes for the victors, gave these Athenian youth, who were in the meantime imprisoned in the Labyrinth and that the victor in the first games was the man who had the greatest power at that time under Minos, and was his general, Taurus by name, who was not reasonable and gentle in his disposition, but treated the Athenian youth with arrogance and cruelty."[17]

The excessively harsh tribute the mythological king exacted from Athens for the "death of his son" represents the harsh tributes the empire demanded of its confederacy–especially of those who rebelled against it–and the actions of Theseus can be attributed to the war and the ultimate collapse of Minoan rule in the Mediterranean. After defeating Minos's "Taurus," Theseus's story parallels the peace treaty enacted between the two cities ca. 1400 BCE by "marrying the heiress" to the throne, and his subsequent abandonment of Ariadne, the "heiress," on Naxos is explained away as being necessary to ensure the continuation of the matrilineal line of succession at Knossos. If any Minoan "priestess-queen" was to accompany her husband to Athens–that is, out of "Minoan" territory–she would lose all rights to the throne of Knossos. It seems a little unlikely that Ariadne would have chosen that fate, but such is the patriarchal nature of mythography.

The Labyrinth

Aside from the symbolism of the bull, there is another obvious recurring symbol: the Labyrinth. Sir Arthur Evans believed that this "labyrinth" was simply the complex system of rooms, ante-rooms, chambers, and halls that made up the palace at Knossos. He believed it was named as such after the main symbol of the double-headed axe of Cretan sovereignty and religion.[18] This axe, or *"labys,"* symbolized the waxing and waning moon joined together back-to-back, representing both the creative and destructive power of the goddess.[19] Aside from the complexity of the palace, archaeologists discovered a real labyrinthine "dance floor" outside the main complex of rooms at Knossos, which at very least created a lasting symbol for the difficulties Athenian raiders might have encountered there. This "labyrinth" is also present in the Theseus myth beyond the episode with the Minotaur, namely at Delos.

The myth states that after he sacrificed to Apollo, Theseus introduced a dance that he had learned during his time at Knossos "which consisted of measured steps in labyrinthine movements." It is believed that the purpose of the labyrinthine floor discovered by archaeologists

---

[17] Pliny *Theseus* 16.1
[18] see Graves 1955 p.297
[19] ibid.

was to facilitate the dance Theseus had "introduced" at Delos. It may seem far-fetched to presume that a dance could find such cultural significance, but wider geographical evidence produces some fascinating results. Graves records similar "dance mazes" further afield in southeastern Europe, the "Beaker B" area of Scandinavia, and northeastern Russia. The Romans also introduced a similar dance in Britain, which is represented in the Welsh *Caer-droia,* a name meaning "Troy-Town," a popular English nomenclature for the turf-mazes found across its isles.

In some dances, the dancers even held a line of cord to ensure they kept the perfect distance between them in their steps. This, Graves suggests, is the possible origin for the magical ball of thread given to Theseus. [20] Speaking of four principal "labyrinths" in his own time, Pliny would appear to agree: "There is still in Egypt, in the Nome of Heracleopolites, a labyrinth, which was the first constructed, three thousand six hundred years ago, they say, by King Petesuchis or Tithöes…That Daedalus took this for the model of the Labyrinth which he constructed in Crete, there can be no doubt; though he only reproduced the hundredth part of it, that portion, namely, which encloses circuitous passages, windings, and inextricable galleries which lead to and fro. We must not, comparing this last to what we see delineated on our mosaic pavements, or to the mazes formed in the fields for the amusement of children, suppose it to be a narrow promenade along which we may walk for many miles together; but we must picture to ourselves a building filled with numerous doors, and galleries which continually mislead the visitor, bringing him back, after all his wanderings, to the spot from which he first set out. This Labyrinth is the second, that of Egypt being the first. There is a third in the Isle of Lemnos, and a fourth in Italy."[21]

Homer also alludes to what the Cretan Labyrinth was and for whom it was built:

"Daedalus in Knossos once contrived

A dancing-floor for fair haired Ariadne."[22]

The Labyrinth may well have been part of the funeral games dedicated to mythical figure Androgeus and the Athenian youths may have been confused with the youths dancing atop the beautiful labyrinthine dance floor at the palace as part of said games. Unfortunately, the details are lost and until the Linear A texts are translated, there appears little possibility of scholars discovering the exact details of the floor's true purpose.

Cult

Another recurrence in the Theseus myth is that of the establishment and suppression of various cults across Bronze Age Greece, and the labors of Theseus supply curious examples. The details of the murder of Sciron, for example, replicate the ritualistic practices the Scirophoria.[23] In this

---

[20] 1955 p.297
[21] Pliny The Elder *The Natural History* 36.19
[22] *Iliad xviii. 592*
[23] Graves 1955 p.311

festival, a "sacred king" was thrown from a cliff as a way of marking the dissolution of the old year.

In another version of the myth, Theseus re-dedicates the Isthmian Games to both Sinis and Sciron after their deaths. Graves records that "Pityocamptes" (the nickname of Sinis) was also the name of a north-westerly wind (as was Sciron) associated with the Boreas cult in Athens. By defeating both of these "villains" the contemporary reader and/or listener might be reminded of the suppression of this cult throughout Attica.[24]

It is the suppression of a cult that gives meaning to the labor of the killing of the Crommyonian Sow. This hunting of a deranged animal amidst four murders may seem a little misplaced until the connection is made between the Crommyonian Sow and the white sow of Demeter. The cult of the "Earth-Goddess" was suppressed in this region, and Graves makes the connection between this suppression, the Sow, and the expulsion of Medea–the witch who used the plants and grains of the earth for her own wicked means–from Athens and Corinth.

The murder of Cercyon is a typical myth of power succession, echoing the myth of Heracles wrestling Antaeus for a kingdom. In this episode, the reader is given a clear example of Theseus's cunning, and how he was actually the inventor of the methods and skills necessary in wrestling, a prized event at all the festival games in ancient Greece, including those he was supposed to have dedicated to Sinis and Sciron.

Thus, in a relatively short series of episodes Theseus is presented as the dominant hero, the suppressor of false cults, and the inventor of practices considered benevolent by Athens mythographers.

The Moon-Goddess

Most religious imagery excavated at Knossos shows women in what has been interpreted as either religious ceremonies or depicted as goddesses. A goddess (often wielding thrashing snakes in either hand) appears in most religious and royal iconography but the appearances of women in Minoan art outweigh those of men in both number and variety of symbolism.[25] This has led scholars to maintain Sir Arthur Evans' conclusions of there being an exalted goddess cult at Knossos, particularly that of a "Moon-Goddess."

In the myth of Theseus, this "Moon-Goddess" appears frequently. Graves states that the imagery of the abduction of Europa is one repeated for many generations and across many Hellenic cults. It is the image of the "Moon-Goddess," riding triumphantly atop the "Sun Cow" who, in some cultures, is depicted as her victim–just as Asterius was Ariadne's victim.[26] In this myth readers are immediately greeted with both bovine and lunar symbolism, strands of meaning

---

[24] ibid.
[25] Koehl 1995
[26] 1955 p.197

that run deeply through the rest of the story.

In his famous *Description of Greece* written in the 2nd century CE, Pausanias explicitly states Pasiphaë is not only connected with the moon, but by his time, her name had come to be "a title of the Moon."[27] Naturally, Pausanias was writing many centuries after the Minoan period, but it is not difficult to imagine that either the myth originally had this meaning or came to adopt it over the centuries. Either way, by the 2nd century CE, readers of this myth would have understood the lunar resonance inherent within.

Graves goes on to connect the story of Pasiphaë and the bull as a ritual marriage between the "Moon-Priestess" and the "Minos-King" who was most often connected to the white bull, an animal sacred to the Moon that Minos couldn't bring himself to sacrifice. Just as the Minoan kingship put no emphasis on individual names of monarchs, but instead, emphasized the cyclical nature of royal succession, the mythical generations of Europa and Pasiphaë repeat the Moon-Goddess and bull symbolism in the myth.

The next generation of "Moon-Goddess" is represented by Ariadne. According to Graves, Ariadne was known by the Greeks as "Ariagne," meaning "very holy," yet another title of the "Moon-Goddess." Theseus's marriage to her–even in the symbolic sense by giving her the jeweled crown he had brought up from the depths–meant Theseus's ascension to the throne of Knossos. He became the "Minos" in that moment. Unsurprisingly, labyrinths were common motifs on coinage found at Knossos, and in one instance, there is the sign of the "new moon" at the center of this motif.[28] If it was Theseus's (the Athenian) task to kill the "Minos" (the Minoan King) at the center of the labyrinthine structure at Knossos, then this new moon could signify the transition of power hinted at within the myth, the revolt of a suppressed people against its tribute-demanding imperial overlord, resulting in an attack on its capital and the possible death and usurpation of its king. Usurpation, that is, with an inherent "divine right," for without the help of Ariadne–the "most holy" or "most powerful" "Moon-Goddess"–Theseus would no doubt have perished within the halls of that dreaded maze.

The Meaning

"The Hero is symbolical of that divine creative and redemptive image which is hidden within us all only waiting to be known and rendered into life." - Joseph Campbell

The most famous work of the celebrated mythologist and writer Joseph Campbell is undoubtedly his *Hero With A Thousand Faces*, a work of comparative mythology that is the culmination of a lifetime of cross-cultural studies into world myth and its socio-cultural and psychological importance. Out of Campbell's extensive work came his theory of the "monomyth," the theory that all myths in all cultures fit, however loosely, into a framework of

---

[27] Pausanias *Description of Greece* iii.26.1
[28] Graves 1955 p.347

critical moments reproduced in modern day stories told on the page and the screen. These moments are broken down into three sections:

The Departure

- The Call to Adventure
- Refusal of the Call
- Supernatural Aid
- The Crossing of the First Threshold
- The Belly of the Whale

Trials and Victories of Initiation

- The Road of Trials
- The Meeting with the Goddess
- Woman as Temptress
- Atonement with the Father
- Apotheosis
- The Ultimate Boon

The Return and Reintegration with Society

- Refusal of the Return
- The Magic of Flight
- Rescue from Without
- Crossing of Return Threshold
- Master of the Two Worlds
- Freedom to Live

Naturally, not all stories contain every stage of the monomyth. Some stories may contain only a bare skeleton of this structure, and as they represent pivotal moments in human lives, the stages do not have to be sequential. The average person must receive dozens of "Calls to Adventure" on a weekly basis and an equal amount of "Refusals" of those calls each time the "necessities" of modern life are given precedence over spiritual growth. However, if examined carefully, every story–be it myth or movie–will eventually bare its soul in the form of these stages.

The myth of Theseus, analyzed through the lens of the monomyth, features at least two "Calls to Adventure" and an inordinate amount of '"Supernatural Aid," but it could be argued that he never progresses beyond the "Apotheosis," due to the choices made by the hero at its center. Theseus doesn't return with the Ultimate Boon" to enrich mankind (unless that "boon" is considered the absence of tribute), and he embraces his return to society like an adolescent who dreams of becoming king.

Fairly self-explanatory, the '"Call" is the catalyst of the hero's predestined adventure. It is the first stage of the mythological journey and it "signifies that destiny has summoned the hero and transferred his spiritual centre[sic] of gravity from within the pale of his society to a zone unknown."[29]

In the case of Theseus, there are at least two "Calls." The first occurs when his mother takes him to the stone–under which his absent father has left him his sword and sandals–and she tells him the story of his birth. This is the moment when Theseus–at the age of 16, when "Calls"' often arrive in droves–decides to step onto the "more dangerous road" in search of his father and his destiny as a hero to rival his cousin, Heracles.

The second comes when he arrives in Athens. He has emerged cleansed and triumphant from his "Trials" and regaling his father with his exploits when a demand for tribute arrives from the Cretan king in the "Great Year," that moment succeeding the traditional eight-year term on the throne, the year in which the king had either to sacrifice himself to make way for the new or find a substitute to fulfill the preordained "death" in his stead. Although Theseus never refuses a "call," there is a "Refusal" in this myth, that of Minos. As Frazer noted, "The bull sacrifice required of King Minos implied that he would sacrifice himself, according to the pattern of the inherited tradition, at the close of his eight-year term. But he seems to have offered, instead, the substitute of the Athenian youths and maidens. That perhaps is how the divine Minos became the monster Minotaur."[30]

Theseus is "called" by destiny to transfer his "spiritual center" from his new, welcoming home at Athens to the "zone unknown" in Crete in order to right the wrong committed by Minos and restore the balance and transference of power. "For the mythological hero is the champion not of things become but of things becoming; the dragon to be slain by him is precisely the monster of the status quo."[31]

Whether it's an enchanted sword or a Babylon Candle, the chosen hero invariably receives supernatural aid when he needs it most, and in ancient Greek myths, the examples of gods bestowing boons on their favorites are legion. A cursory reading of Homer's *Iliad* will prove as much. This "Aid" can come in the form of an object or an evasion, influence the people surrounding the hero, or come from the hero's own physical capabilities, but it will come.

Throughout his story, Theseus is painted as a favorite of the gods. From the Arthurian retrieval of the sword in the stone to the image of Aphrodite that bewitched Ariadne, Theseus was touched by the supernatural whose aid represents the benign, protecting power, destiny.[32] Daedalus learned his craft from Athena and so the ball of string he gave to Ariadne, which subsequently saved Theseus's life, is the supernatural aid undiluted from its passage through hands to its chosen receiver.[33] Theseus intuitively *knows* his destiny is preordained and he trusts

---

[29] Campbell 2008 p.48
[30] 1922 p. 280
[31] Campbell 2008 p. 289
[32] Campbell 2008 p. 59

he will receive aid from the gods whenever he needs it. In other words, Theseus portrays the need for–and ultimate reward of–*hope*.

The crossing of the first threshold is the most dangerous part of the adventure. If the call hasn't been answered, then this threshold will never be seen. If the call is answered, however, then there is no turning back. As Joseph Campbell put it, "The adventure is always and everywhere a passage beyond the veil of the known into the unknown; the powers that watch at the boundary are dangerous; to deal with them risky; yet, for anyone with competence and bravery, the danger fades."[34]

Theseus knew there were bandits on the road but had no idea of the dangers he would face. When he took up the call to exact equal justice to the crime, he said he would choose no quarrel but accept the divine role he had brought upon himself. This was his cousin's way and he would honour the most lauded hero of his day by following in his footsteps.

By stepping out on the "more dangerous route," Theseus caused a ripple in the pond that would change the universe, with him at its epicenter. His destiny is the destiny of all Athenians, though they didn't know it at the time. When it came for him to answer the second call–that which came from Crete–he had never been to the island and had never faced a monster so ferocious, yet his choice to step aboard the ship would be the defining moment in every Athenian's life up until that point. Athens is the "world," according to the ancient reader of Theseus's myth, not simply because it was the primary city in Greece (though it would later rise to such esteem). By comparison, "Athens" could easily be replaced with "Faerie," "Narnia," or "Middle Earth." What Athens represented was the cosmos, everyday life at the complete mercy of the hero brave and competent enough to risk everything to protect her.

According to Campbell, the "Belly of the Whale" represents the "awesome power of the womb" which, interestingly, is universal to all myths.[35] Heracles at Troy, Raven on the shores of the Bering Strait, Odin hanging from the World Tree–all heroes must immerse themselves in an abyss from which they cannot escape until they have experienced a transformative "death." According to Christian tradition, Jesus spent the same amount of time in the tomb–three days–as Jonah did in the "Great Fish." Both emerged changed; their removal from the "world" in a "mini-death" is what ultimately made them heroes.

Theseus enters the "Belly" on a number of occasions; although the road he took from Troezen to Athens was a "Road of Trials," it was also the "Belly of the Whale." He emerged from that road and those transformative dangers, not as the 16-year old imitator but as a real hero. Before he could return to society he needed to finalize his transformation; he needed to be reborn. Here, the mythographers placed the sons of Phytalus at the river Cephissus to wash away the sins he

---

[33] Graves 1955 p. 313
[34] 2008 pp. 67-68
[35] 2005 p. 77

had committed in the "Belly" and to allow him to enter the city of his father in glory, ready to accept his future call.

The second "Belly" into which Theseus entered was, of course, the labyrinth. The "Belly" strips all would-be heroes of any vanities and forces him to become "annihilated" in his metamorphosis. Although the ball of thread is attached to the limen, it does not help the hero face his dangers inside the labyrinth, because for that he will need to depend on his competence and will. In most versions of the myth, Theseus kills the Minotaur with his bare hands, a nod toward the cousin he hoped to emulate (Heracles had killed the Nemean Lion in the same way), but it's also a sign that he (literally) wrestled with his inner-self and arose victorious.

The road of trials is possibly the most important moment in the adventure of the hero. Here, he experiences a baptism by fire, searing away the ego in order to fulfill Destiny's expectations. In adolescence, childish preoccupations are laid behind and the hero prepares to confront the true face of the cosmos and all the dangers and tests that lie therein. "The is the 'purification of the self;' by concentrating our energies and interests on transcendental things we dissolve, transcend and transmute the infantile images of our personal past…this ordeal is the deepening of the problem of the First Threshold. The question is still in the balance: can the ego put itself to death?"

In the case of Theseus, the "Road" is both figurative and literal. On the way to Athens he is faced with "Trials" he feels destined to confront, leaving justice in his wake. This is the real test of the hero, but it is also the moment he has been waiting for as well. While discussing "Supernatural Aid," Joseph Campbell quotes Napoleon Bonaparte at the opening of his Russian campaign in a way that is enlightening when reflecting on the hero's motivations behind embarking on the perilous "Road": "I feel myself driven towards an end that I do not know. As soon as I shall have reached it, as soon as I shall become unnecessary, an atom will suffice to shatter me. Till then, not all the forces of mankind can do anything against me."[36]

The self-assuredness of the hero on his "Road' is what drives him forward, so certain of his destiny that he will happily volunteer to be offered as tribute to the Minotaur. He knows that nothing–not even the monstrous beast at the center of the impossible labyrinth–will prevent him from performing what the Cosmos has set forth for him. Theseus never doubts he can kill the Minotaur despite the fact he has no prior evidence of his being able to do so. He doesn't need prior evidence; it is his destined future.

Here is where the story of Theseus begins to unravel in terms of the monomyth. Afterward, he has other "Calls to Adventure" and descends into other "Bellies of Whales" and other "Trials," but he never progresses beyond the "Meeting of the Goddess" and the "Atonement" forced upon him as a result of it.

---

[36] 2008 p.59

Robert Graves believed Theseus may have become a god if Athens had been more powerful and had more cultural sway among the Hellenes, but if the myth is analyzed in terms of the monomyth, there may be another reason for his lack of "Apotheosis." The "Meeting of the Goddess" occurs "when all barriers and ogres have been overcome."[37] Theseus meets Ariadne before entering the labyrinth, but their "sacred union" arrives when he's left victorious after it. She's duplicitous and able, made obvious by the conspiracy against her family and her part in ensuring the death of her half-brother. Her power as "Moon-Goddess" is attested by her lineage. Theseus was unwise to make an oath to her as if she were an ordinary girl, since she is the "Mother Goddess." As such, "she encompasses all: good, bad, fear, safety. She is the cosmos, terrible in her abilities, benevolent in our desperate eyes…the hero who can take her as she is, without undue commotion but with the kindness and assurance she requires is potentially the king, the incarnate god, of her created world."[38]

After all Ariadne had sacrificed for him, by leaving her on the island, Theseus refused the goddess and the results were terrible, divine, and inevitable. It was she who called upon the gods to punish the victorious hero, and they did so in a way that bridged two critical moments in the monomyth: the "Meeting of the Goddess" and "Atonement with the Father." When Aegeus threw himself from the Acropolis as a result of the wrath of the "Goddess," Theseus's fate of atonement was realized. "To the son, the Father represents the future task,"[39] but the future task is to become "At One" with the father. Ariadne's wrath forced Theseus to replace him, and although the difference may be slight according to Joseph Campbell's psychoanalytical investigation, it is an important robbery, as "accepting this At-One-Ment is the key to bliss."[40] By robbing Theseus of this moment, it could be argued that he was never allowed to find the "bliss" all heroes ultimately seek. After all of his trials and adventures, he refused the "Goddess" and was forced to become the "unquiet King" whose ascension to the throne is simply another moment in a cyclical repetition of the stages that had already come before. He fought centaurs and was imprisoned in the Underworld, and he married an Amazon and was tricked by the gods into killing his own son – "Trials" and "Bellies," "Bellies" and "Trials" – until he was eventually thrown off a cliff on the island of Skyros after losing the love of his people.

Although Theseus came to a brutal end, this is not the emphasis of the myth. All of his trials, both before and after his awful treatment of Ariadne, were glorified as the feats of the divinely chosen. He would continue to be a shining, national symbol for the city of Athens for centuries after he was adopted as such during the Persian Wars, and his story is one of struggle and attainment and of divine love and destiny. In the end, it's still the story of a Hero.

At the same time, in this beloved myth, Theseus not only represents Athens but also the common Athenian, and thus the common human. Every person on the planet is living his or her

---

[37] Campbell 2008 p. 91
[38] ibid. p. 97
[39] Campbell 2008 p. 110
[40] ibid.

own adventure–this is the meaning of *The Hero with a Thousand Faces*–and he or she can look to Theseus and other heroes for inspiration, for reassurance that their efforts will be vindicated, and to avoid the follies and failures leading to their tribulations. Readers are told that each acceptance of a "Call to Adventure" will be met with the "Supernatural Aid" needed to fulfill his or her own destiny. Master storyteller Paulo Coehlo understood this power of mythology when he wrote, "When you want something, all the universe conspires in helping you to achieve it."

Online Resources

Other books about ancient history by Charles River Editors

Other books about ancient Greece by Charles River Editors

Other books about Theseus and the Minotaur on Amazon

Bibliography

Antoninus Liberalis (1992) Metamorphoses trans. Francis Celoria Psychology Press

Campbell, J. (2008) The Hero With A Thousand Faces University of Princeton Frazer, J. G. (1922) The Golden Bough Macmillan

Gaius Valerius Catullus (1894) The Carmina trans. Leonard C. Smithers London.

Graves, R., 1955 The Greek Myths Penguin

Homer (1924) The Iliad trans A.T. Murray, Ph.D. in two volumes. Cambridge, MA., Koehl, R.B. (1995) The Nature of Minoan Kingship. In: Rehak, P. (ed.): The Role of Pliny the Elder (1855)The Natural History. John Bostock, M.D., F.R.S. H.T. Riley, Esq., B.A. London. Taylor and Francis

Harvard University Press

Pausanias (1918) Description of Greece trans. W.H.S. Jones, Litt.D., and H.A. Ormerod, M.A., in 4 Volumes. Cambridge, MA, Harvard University Press

Plutarch. Plutarch's Lives. trans. Bernadotte Perrin. Cambridge, MA. Harvard University Press.

K. Anne Pyburn 2004 Ungendering Civilization Psychology Press

the Ruler in the Prehistoric Aegean. Aegaeum 11 pp. 23-35

Rehak, P. (1855) (ed.): The Role of Pliny the Elder The Natural History. John Bostock, M.D., F.R.S. H.T. Riley, Esq., B.A. London. Taylor and Francis

Free Books by Charles River Editors

We have brand new titles available for free most days of the week. To see which of our titles are currently free, click on this link.

Discounted Books by Charles River Editors

We have titles at a discount price of just 99 cents everyday. To see which of our titles are currently 99 cents, click on this link.

Printed in Great Britain
by Amazon